The Family Book Society
Anthology 1

TELEPEN

D0784428

The Poetry Book Society Anthology 1 New Series

Edited by
Fraser Steel

Hutchinson
London Sydney Auckland Johannesburg

© in this collection The Poetry Book Society 1990.
The copyright of the individual poems remains with the authors.

All rights reserved

This edition first published in 1990 by Hutchinson Ltd, an imprint of Century
Hutchinson Ltd, Random Century House, 20 Vauxhall Bridge Road, London
SW1V 2SA, and by the Poetry Book Society Ltd, 21 Earls Court Square,
London SW5

Century Hutchinson Australia (Pty) Ltd
20 Alfred Street, Milsons Point, Sydney,
NSW 2061 Australia

Century Hutchinson New Zealand Ltd
PO Box 40–086, Glenfield, Auckland 10,
New Zealand

Century Hutchinson South Africa (Pty) Ltd
PO Box 337, Bergvlei, 2012 South Africa

A CIP catalogue record for this book is available from the British Library

0 09 174323 0

Set in Times by ⋔ Tek Art Ltd
Printed and bound in Great Britain by Cox and Wyman Ltd, Reading

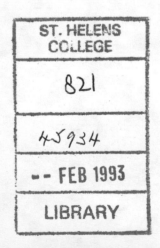

ST. HELENS
COLLEGE

821

45934

-- FEB 1993

LIBRARY

Contents

Introduction

The way to keep out of trouble when assembling an anthology like this is to arrange the poets alphabetically. I'd better explain why I've opted for trouble.

For ten years or so I was at the receiving end of most of the poetry manuscripts sent to the BBC. The postbag was too miscellaneous to prompt many generalisations, but one thought which persistently surfaced was that the readiest supply of the refreshing and the unexpected seemed to come from the edges of the British Isles. In a sense this was a bit of an illusion: the London-Oxford-Cambridge triangle is still the main bourse of reputations, and much of what reached me from there had already been given the face of familiarity by the activities of publishers and critics. Nevertheless, differences kept asserting themselves.

At the same time, I was becoming increasingly aware of a refreshment of the language of English poetry from writers in other English-speaking lands – Derek Walcott in the Caribbean, Allen Curnow in New Zealand, Chinua Achebe in Nigeria, Margaret Atwood in Canada, as well as the thundering horde of Americans.

We shouldn't build too much on these differences: English, like Latin, is the name of a language, and, wherever it is written, the poetry in that language must, as C.H. Sisson has argued, come ultimately to the same judgement. Who, Sisson asks, would regard Martial as a Spanish poet? But until that last judgement, when George Herbert and William Carlos Williams will be folded in a single piece, the differences are of interest. They are perhaps more cultural than poetic, but where cultural differences encompass different styles of using or inhabiting the language they go pretty close to the root of the matter of poetry – and they have their relevance to the poetry of these islands.

I have arranged the anthology in four sections: Scotland, England, Ireland, Wales – not to make any particular assertion, and still less to instigate unseemly competition. I simply want to raise the question of what the diversity of our contemporary poetry may owe to the four distinct national and literary traditions which in some measure underlie it. The question is complicated by the fact that three of the four have roots which are to some degree Celtic and, tenuous though those roots may now be, it would be a mistake to ignore them. Even in Scotland, where the numerical decline of the language has been almost as steep as its devoutest enemy could wish, a Gaelic poet such as Sorley MacLean has been able to penetrate the imagination of his English-speaking contemporaries, and I have thought it important to include at least a few reminders of the vitality of Celtic literary traditions whose very existence, against the pressures of history, should be a wonder to us. I have also borne in mind the arrival in English poetry of other voices, some from what used to be called the Empire, some from the wider world, which are offering, it seems to me, both challenges and possibilities of renewal to the domestic product.

Assigning poets to their 'proper' sections has been a bit of a problem – Hadrian's Wall has been permeable for some time now, Offa's Dyke no longer performs its intended function, the Holyhead Ferry keeps to a regular schedule, and what does one do about resident Americans and New Zealanders? I have taken a short way with the hard cases: some have been given their choice of billet, some have been assigned on the basis of their postal address. The product of such difficulties, as well as the constraints of space and the limitations of the editor's own taste, is a book which will almost certainly leave every reader convinced that an injustice has been done to someone or other. If there is one injustice I am conscious of, it is towards England (and who more deserving of it, cries the chorus of Celts). But there she is, predominant, certainly, and a little neglectful of some of the cherished sensibilities of the rest of us, yet still comparatively tolerant of cultural presences which most other nations would regard as threats to their identity, and never permitted a legitimate nationalism of her own.

But the questions I want the anthology to raise are about nationality, not nationalism. A book of this kind can hardly do more than indicate some of them, and I don't claim to have answered any. One thing is certain, however: with the EEC accelerating the pace of integration even as the countries of Central and Eastern Europe begin to recover (for good or ill) their sense of what it is to be a nation, it will not be the last word on the subject.

One editorial point. Readers may notice that the arrangement of the sections corresponds with the final order of the 1990 Rugby Union home international tournament. Even-handedness is all very well, and it is perhaps the least I owe to the poets who have been good enough to contribute their work: but I am, after all, a Scot of the Diaspora, and the hem (as that considerable London Scot, Thomas Carlyle noted) is stouter than the cloth.

Fraser Steel

SCOTLAND

ROBERT CRAWFORD

Chevalier

The voice is holed-up in a cave. Water drips on it. Silent,
Despised men keep watch outside.

The voice in the heather, disguised as a woman, moves
Mostly at night. Money's available

For information about the voice. Vessels
Wait all day offshore, listening.

The voice is nearly inaudible on a tiny island. Sun beats
    down on its vowels.
People are burned out for the voice, which sheds

Enough clothes for many generations. They festoon
    museums.
It gets so quiet searchers hear nothing,

Can't even tell its language. The voice escapes
To Argentina and Cape Breton Island, gets drunk,

Mouthing obscenities, toasting itself
Over and over. Silence doesn't chasten it.

Rewards and spies increase. The voice
Loses consciousness, won't be betrayed.

RUARAIDH MACTHÒMAIS

Freud

An aillse a' criomadh
a' charbaird iarainn ud,
a' tolladh anns a' chnàimh,
's an eanchainn a' strì
ris an dealbh a dhèanamh coimhlionta
a thòisich a' fàs
beag air bheag anns a' bhrù chian sin
mus do bhlais e cìoch a mhàthar,
mus tàinig sgàile athar air àrainn;
na ceallan bàsail a' sgaoileadh
ann an ìochdar an aodainn,
an smiogaid ga chreachadh,
a' bruthadh an smuain
a bha a' ruith anns an fhuil dhearg sin
fad ficheadan bliadhna,
's a chaidh bhon uair sin
ann an eanchainn an t-saoghail,
a' sgaoileadh 's a' milleadh 's a' slànadh.

Freud
(Translated by the author under his foreign name of Derick Thomson)

Cancer nibbling
at that iron jaw,
digging into the bone,
while the brain struggles
to complete the picture
that began to grow
little by little in that distant womb
before he tasted his mother's breast,
before his father's shadow fell;
the deadly cells proliferating
in the lower part of the face,
the chin shattered,
pressing in on the thought that ran
in that red blood for scores of years,
and has gone since then
into the brain of the world,
spreading and spoiling and healing.

IAIN CRICHTON SMITH

Macbeth and the Witches

When the sun was white and drained of energy
Macbeth met the witches under the rim of the sky.
'Why did you confirm my evil?' he said.

And the witches who were lighting thorns in the cold winter
        said,
'There is a play that one plays when the summer is over
and you happened to be one of the cards in our hand,

a deformed king, with a coat too large for him,
and a crown that sizzled in the white wintry sky.
These things after a while are not important

Except to those who suffer, who are not important.
Feeling belongs to the spring and the ignorance of lovers.
Here in this wood it is a question of passing the time,

and the abstract intellect constructs dramas
with a queen and some pawns and the immortal joker
who faces both ways at the frosty January gates.

Let be, let be. It was quite a nice structure.
And truth after all can be played with under this sun
which is fading slowly towards a renaissance of leaves.

Come join us, join us, at the unimportant edge of things,
wearing your coat of blood with the hole in the breast.
This is the west. The east has innocent wings.'

Halloween

This small child has an old man's face,
an old man's clayey bleak unquestioning face.
He plays the violin and sings a song,
small, expressionless, unquestioning.

And then, after he has played, he pulls
the mask away, and there he stands
fresh-faced and laughing with blond curls
and from the grave extends his hands.

As a Guest

As a guest who troubles you by staying too long
and who is found awkwardly in rooms or studying books
aslant to the house and its usual presences,
so it may be that we too will feel this –

our trouble to the earth, inarticulate with age,
creating more turmoil than our lives should warrant,
tremulous haunters of toilets and of bedrooms –
waiting for that definite lenient stroke.

NORMAN MacCAIG

The Red and the Black

We sat up late, talking –
thinking of the screams of the tortured
and the last silence of starving children,
seeing the faces of bigots and murderers.

Then sleep.

And there was the morning, smiling
in the dance of everything. The collared doves
guzzled the rowan berries and the sea
washed in, so gently, so tenderly.
Our neighbours greeted us
with humour and friendliness.

World, why do you do this to us,
giving us poison with one hand
and the bread of life with another?

And reason sits helpless at its desk,
adding accounts that never balance,
finding no excuse for anything.

GRAHAM FULTON

Old Haunt

An ID parade of flaking angels.
We try to visit your Mother's grave
but you can't remember where you left her,
when you were here last, four years ago.

Nothing seems the same, you say.

The wire-mesh bins are choked with petals,
plastic bottles, daffodil wrap.
A blown-over flowerpot bumps along gravel,
a soft white rabbit cuddles a stone.
EMMA   NINE MONTHS   DEARLY LOVED.

And your tears fill the rain as you scrape
down deep
through turf and earth enclosing your mind
for a glimpse of a half-remembered image.
Brooding CIBA-GEIGY PIGMENTS. Boarded mill,
flats and stacks. View of the town buried in silence
except for the roar of the three o'clock crowd.

Town of your birth, town of her death

this woman I met in a box of old snapshots,
dressed for work or longskirt dances,
milking cows on an Irish farm
in Wellington boots and a knitted hat,
hair glowing black then butterfly-white

at the turn of a Kodak, blink of an eye.

One hour on and there she is
on the same row we walked down one hour ago.
Six limp stalks in your hand. Hair plastered
to our skulls.

Nothing, you say, seems the same.

The wire-mesh bins are choked with hymnsheets,
chestnut branches have been hacked back.

FRANK KUPPNER

Odysseus: A Node

1 From the ocean liner of my body, which
   still seems to be fairly seaworthy on the
   troublefree rims of the deep – sheltered bays,
   rivermouths, inlets, all such boring places,
   (much of the more elaborate navigational
   equipment was abandoned to the storms
   of my last few trips on the ocean) – I looked out
   at so much building still going on in the shipyards
   and at last understood what they were doing.

2 They are building a replica of you, Penelope.
   Of astonishing size. Much like you ought to be.

3 Yes; I believe the eventual plan
   is to replace the Statue of Liberty
   (that very big girl) with yourself, Eleutheria.

4 You will be fully clothed, of course, Enchantress.
   How many disasters at sea that should prevent!

5 Needless to say, you will no longer be known as the
   Statue of Liberty. More like the opposite, in fact. The
   simplest reason for this I can give you is that there will
   probably no longer be anyone on Earth, apart from me.
   And, as my navigational equipment (I think I may have
   already mentioned this) has been rendered so faulty by
   repeated shocks, I could be anywhere.

6 But I am definitely somewhere, Sexybum, have no fear of
      that.

ANDREW GREIG

Widow & Moon

The moon is hung
over the flyover,
wraps round the throat
of the widow as she drives
sound way up loud, courage,
that wheel, firmly in both hands.

Smiling by God and minding.

The moon's set off, she'd say,
by that black cloud,
and you do find
this lop-sided smile
kinda sexy, hmm?
I drive most nights,
and it helps to find
between here and there
there are no bogles.
No one knows, not even me
how close to home I am.

The moon has her by the throat
and she puts her foot down,
flickering flat out over the Forth.

Essaouira

We always knew there'd be a place
where North Atlantic winds converge
on Africa as we went down
for sardines and cigarettes among the nets
with Hervé, Yassim, Mr James,
and after work there would be time
for mint tea and talk in the Place Moulay Hassan
where women in haik sat like pillars of salt
and hooded men strolled hand in hand
by children rapt on the mosaics . . .

We knew dusk must adjust its shawl
by the Red Cafe, round the hammam,
and desert winds disturb those birds
hung in their cages in the hall;
now all we've said and done will be
blown over the ocean without adieu –
the residue glitters as salt on the tiles
and our eyes bear the sheen of windows facing the sea.

GEORGE MACKAY BROWN

The Rackwick Dove

A pigeon was hurled from its course
Into the valley of salt and corn. . . .

Will it leap over the hill's shoulder again?
Ah, it hasn't the strength.

Bide awhile then, bird of peace
About the thresholds of Rackwick.

The bird hesitates between sixteen gables.
Too many crofts are empty skulls.

Go, there's Lucy up at Glen.
Lucy will scatter you crumbs galore.

The knight of music, up at Bunertoon, Sir Peter,
All birds are his friends. Fly there.

Twenty children of summer on the beach.
One could make a salt branch of her arm.

On Mucklehoose roof it flutters, falls.
Hutch has hammered a fish-box house.

Alan threw grain on the flagstones.
It lives like a prince on gold tithes.

But it pined for the broken flight,
Longed for the lost grey company.

After breakfast, one morning, we find
It has shaken our abundant salt from its wings.

EDWIN MORGAN

A Defence

I am told I should not love him, the magpie,
that he's a bully, but then I watch them bouncing
along the grass, chattering, black and white and
he and she, twigs in beak, the tree-top swaying
with half a nest in a hail-shower, the magpies
seeing off crows and gulls – a feint of mobbing
but who knows – eyeing a lost swan waddling
down the pavement, off course from Bingham's waters,
the smart bright bold bad pairing caring magpies
whose nest was blown down last December, back now
to build again, to breed again, to bring us
a batch of tumbling clockwork liquorice allsorts,
spruce, spliced, diced, learning to prance and hurtle
through evening and morning sycamores with what must be
something like happiness, the magpies, cocky,
hungry, handsome, an eye-catching flash for that
black and white collie to bark at, and the black and
white cat lurking under the car-bonnet
to lash a bushy tail at, and this page, seeing
these things, first white, now white and black, to pay its
tribute to, and lay out, thus, its pleasure.

A Skew

They proved the theory of surplus matter
by finding almost infinitely tiny
traces of the pipe the universe was
blown from, like a vase in Venice. Fragments
ranging through a dozen constellations
gave out at last a strangely twisted oval,
as if the blower had once been a jailbird,
blew as he spoke, with half his mouth. Onward,
the astronomers cried, fine, who needs a circle?
Better to live like flies in a bashed rummer
sweetened with fresh beer-dregs and froth-splotches
than skate a smiling perfect disc – incisive –
twice – three times – and drown. So they made merry
in orbit and on the mountain-tops, preparing
news of the skews, that was the phrase, for broadcast,
leaving the darker question of what prison
the gaunt primordial glassblower had starved in
before escaping to produce such matter
as he'd have wished a hundred times robuster
though not more perfect, if in imperfection
starriest anti-handedness prevailed there.

ENGLAND

IAN McMILLAN

In A West Yorkshire Bus Queue, Several Mature Art Students Discuss Excitedly The Earthquake Of April 2nd 1990

I was leaning against the wall,
phoning my husband/A present from
Polperro, it just fell to the ground,
drifted like a leaf. The light
in St Ives/he works in Oldham and he said

Yes, yes, I can feel it too!

I was in my studio, well I call it/
I ran out on to the lawn to stand,
to experience it and, well, my dear,
I had quite forgotten, quite forgotten

that I always sculpt naked!

my studio, it's really the shed.
The paints ran, I swear the paints
scuttled down the canvas/at first

I covered my breasts up!

I'm working on a new piece,
two people, leaning against walls

miles apart!

PATRICIA BEER

Nailsea Glass

In England in September people go
Indoors, to paintings, glass and porcelain,
Their own or some museum's. Nailsea men
Who worked in glass were much less comme-il-faut

And Christian than their kind but they could blow
Glass far better and they threw a crystal chain
Of objects round the world and back again.
In galleries and at auctions they still glow.

Nailsea do-gooders founded Sunday Schools.
The blowers had their own theology
And called the furnaces Hell Mouth. The flames

That led to drunkenness and nudity
Ended as cool green glass. Their hands and names
Were black, their wares bright as saved souls.

1815

This soldier from his grave declares
That he was nothing but his wars.
His soul was made out of camp-fires.

His tombstone does not say he fought
Simply that he was present at –
And then the battle's name and date.

His name is small, the battle's large.
He was the bayonet and the dirge.
He was the chinstrap and the charge.

A dozen yew trees further on
The memory of his name has gone.
It lingered somewhere with his son.

This way he has become a street,
A bridge, a station, the defeat
That any overlord could meet.

The tombstone is his state of mind.
Now as the evening sun comes round
Something is rising from the ground:

The sweet smell of humility?
For he was present on that day
Yet what he did he does not say.

DAVID WRIGHT

On The River Avon, Near Stratford

He is, of course, the genius of the place,
That is, of midland England, whose flatness
Rescues it from unreasonable beauty;
A pleasant, unremarkable country
Watered by its river Avon, whose source is
The middle point of England, near Naseby.

I knew its reaches well: at least from Evesham
As far as Warwick. Then I was a boy
And it was the summer armadas came over
With the full moon, flying to Birmingham
And back again, unladen, before morning.
I saw the cattle drowsing in the fields,
And black elms ponder over scarcely pacing
Water, while white spokes of light, far off,
Walked on the horizon until All Clear.
And there my boat lay, floating on the water,
Well above Bidford; ready to go on.

The time, like all times, furious; my voyage
Frivolous, without aim, peripheral.
But now I feel its meaning, as I did then,
A realization that a golden age
Exists; at all times, though no age is golden;
And that it is enough to see it once:
A derelict park, receding pastoral,
An intense present, ever caught between
All that must be because of what has been.

ROY FISHER

The Host

This memory, never mind what it is,
breaks in from nowhere with senses charged

and wants me to move over. Over
me it takes precedence. It's in flood.

Nobody but me has this memory.
This memory has nobody but me.

And for thirty-eight years eight months,
not subject, as I've been, to ageing,

it has lodged in me without ever
communicating with me in any way I've been

able to recognize. There's nobody else
it can possibly have been in touch with in all that while

except through me; and I know it's never tried.
Vampire memory, somehow or other feeding off me.

The Poetry Of Place

A resident of Rutherford, New Jersey,
happens to have for sale, at collectors'
price, a wheelbarrow,
old, but not old enough, red,
but too red: painting it up,
he's obviously not seen the shade
quite right. His greed makes him
a hasty reader. Glazed
with varnish, it'll do. Whoever buys it
gets to see the room where the original
things with ideas in them are.

SIMON ARMITAGE

You May Turn Over And Begin . . .

'Which of these films was Dirk Bogarde
not in? One hundredweight of bauxite

makes how much aluminium?
How many tales in *The Decameron*?'

General Studies, the upper sixth, a doddle, a cinch
for anyone with an ounce of common sense

or a calculator
with a memory feature.

Having galloped through but not caring enough
to check or double check, I was dreaming of

milk white breasts and nakedness, or more specifically
virginity.

That term – everybody felt the heat
but the girls were having none of it:

long and cool like cocktails,
out of reach, their buns and pigtails

only let out for older guys with studded jackets
and motor bikes and sparc helmets.

One jot of consolation
was the tall spindly girl riding pillion

on her man's new Honda,
who, with the lights at amber

put down both feet and stood, to stretch her limbs,
to lift the visor and push back her fringe

and to smooth her tight jeans.
As he pulled off down the street

she stood there like a wishbone,
high and dry, her legs wide open

and rumour has it he didn't notice
till he came round in the ambulance

having under balanced on a tight left hander.
A Taste of Honey. Now I remember.

GLYN MAXWELL

Chanson Cordiale

In le green home county of le desperate for nothing,
Fussed in son bedroom whom they all called fool,
While strolled in sa summerthings whom I in secret termed
A real damn fox, and was a real damn fox.

Up la white hillock of les real crap at cricket,
Milled, if you call it that, a curiously many:
Among them in a minute came, checking the team changes,
Him le young and lucky who did not know he was né.

Where in any other ville would you yourself be looking
For the heroine of this but elsewhere? Avec the villains,
Down in the pint-drinking places all the licensed hours, hein?
Not behind la glace framboise and happening to be passing.

Through the clocked après-midi with most of the expected
        things
Hobbling from fruition to the blanche pavilion,
Him du decent home-sweet-home was pointillisting boxes
To note what small espoir there was, what small espoir there
        was.

Yes, unless you count, and il did not or didn't want to,
Eyes of a close female on the good work he was doing.
He could have had half hours of her, and she was free as this is.
Pausing there, hair in the sky so sacré blooming bleu.

But I in public walked to watch at least le close of playing,
Was late, though, so ambled towards my Pimms Numéro 1;
Did, however, on the other red hair-smoothing hand,
Mobilize into the shade where the fox had her back.

On into le soir and she remembered as we darkened, it
Thinned the blue enthusiasts to summery ghosts,
To wasps in the dead glasses, birds where the wickets were,
And threaded the scorer homeward, past mes yeux, past ses
    yeux.

Neither betrayed anything. There may well have been
    nothing
To betray, and anyhow, I topped up her eau
Non-gazeuse. She once asked the name of the aforesaid
Scorer. J'ai repondu 'Je ne sais pas!' though I do.

What would you imagine but that elle to her soirée,
Though fond enough of me, va, and I, not any sleepier,
Head back to the bright town and too many bières à
    pression,
Telling the score and how I am to him and him and him –

That me and her? Hélas, she was a regular damn fox,
And so say I, she put mon tricot over sa summerthings,
Anyhow. I'm for mon lit. Au revoir till autumn!
To le green old county, my home-returning braves.

JOHN WHITWORTH

This Is My Own, My Native Land

At school one Catholic and forty Jews
Were absent at Assembly, and I'd guess
English episcopalians like me could choose
The same sectarian exclusiveness,
But never being one to nurse the bruise

Of difference, I sweated at my text.
'Och aye,' I could say, 'Ye ken,' and 'Whit fer no?'
(Perhaps that last was going a bit far.) Next,
The review of Scottish History's Horrorshow
Left certain ancient loyalties perplexed:

Was Good Queen Bess, the hammer of the Armada,
A conniving, flinty-bosomed, red-haired bitch?
– She was. And were Jacobites good or bad? – Much harder.
Bonnie Dundee killed Presbyterians, which
Was very bad, but Charlie's martial ardour

Losing the scabbard, rightly understood,
Since Southern epicenes are scarcely missed,
Made him a kind of Tartan Robin Hood;
Like the bluff, rugger-playing Nationalist
Kneeing my Sassenach balls in, that was good.

MICHAEL DONAGHY

Fraction

The umpteenth time my mother told the story
Of her cousins dismembered by a British bomb,
I turned on her, her Irish son. 'I'm American.
I was born here.' She went to pieces.

And would not be solaced. I had her eyes,
The aunt's, that is, who, the story goes,
Was brought to the jail to sort the bits in tubs.
Toes. I meant to renounce such grotesque pity.

I was thirteen. I didn't know who I was. She knew.
As I held her wrists, reassuring,
Repeating, that I was her Irish son,
I was the man who'd clicked the toggle switch

Bracing himself between two branches,
Between the flash and the report.

Liverpool

Ever been tattooed? It takes a whim of iron,
takes sweating in the antiseptic-stinking parlour,
nothing to read but motorcycle magazines,
before the blood sopped cotton and, of course, the needle,
all for – at best – some Chinese dragon. Or else its 'MUM'
or 'JESUS'. But mostly they do hearts,

hearts skewered, blurry, spurting like the *Sacre Coeur*,
on the arms of bikers and sailors.
Even in gaol they get by with biro ink and broken glass
carving hearts into their hands and shoulders.
But women's are more intimate. They hide theirs,
under shirts and jeans, in order to bestow them.

Like Tracy, who confessed she'd had hers done
one legless weekend with her ex.
Heart. Arrow. Even the bastard's initials, RJL,
somewhere where it hurt, she said,
and when I asked her where, snapped 'Liverpool'.

Wherever it was, she'd had it sliced away
leaving a scar, she said, pink and glassy,
but small, and better than having his mark on her,

that self same mark of Valentinus,
who was flayed for love, but who never
– so the cardinals now say – existed.
Desanctified, apocryphal, like Christopher,

like the scar you never showed me, Trace,
your (   ), your ex, your 'Liverpool'.
Still, when I unwrap the odd anonymous note,
I let myself believe that it's from you.

WENDY COPE

The Concerned Adolescent

Our planet spins around the sun
in its oval-shaped orbit
like a moth circling a bright, hot, golden-yellow
                                    light bulb.
Look at this beautiful, lovely
blue and green and white jewel
shining against the dark black sky.
It is doomed.

On another planet somewhere far away in the galaxy
beings are discussing the problems of Earth.
'It is a wonderful world,' says their leader,
It has roaring oceans filled with many kinds of
                                    fishes,
It has green meadows bedecked with white and yellow
                                    flowers,
Its trees have twisting roots and fruitful, abundant
                                    branches.
But it is doomed.

'The problem with this lovely, beautiful world, you
                                    see,
Is the inhabitants, known as HUMAN BEINGS.
Human beings will not live in peace and love
and care for the little helpless creatures who share
                        the planet with them.
They pollute the world, they kill and eat the
                                    animals.
Everywhere there is blood and the stench of death.
Human beings make war and hate one another.
They do not understand their young, they reject their
                                    ideals,

they make them come home early from the disco.
They are doomed.'

Soon a great explosion, a terrible cloud
will wipe out all the life on this planet,
including those people who do not see how important
                                    my poem is.
They are certainly doomed.

I Worry

I worry about you –
So long since we spoke.
Love, are you downhearted,
Dispirited, broke?

I worry about you.
I can't sleep at night.
Are you sad? Are you lonely?
Or are you all right?

They say that men suffer,
As badly, as long.
I worry, I worry,
In case they are wrong.

DAVID SCOTT

Wedding

Is there something huge
I have not done
to give this wedding such a push
that it will swing for ever?

What conjuror could squeeze
so many aspirations
through such a small ring?

If I was him
I would want to get out
of these absolutes quicker
than a stiff collar,

get engrossed
in the sacrament of what goes
where in the living room.

Flowers aside,
here is one who's
caught the colour of the sun
this afternoon.

ROBERT STUART

Rosemary's Song

It brings me no pleasure to see
the sun burst in at half
past six, and tell you to
go back to bed, Rosemary, curl

in my back. Where's your sleep?
Where's mine that I had and lost,
pricked on a spindle's needle,
awake forever now

at midnight, the plump moon
between our faces on the pillow,
your face happy and talking.
Where's your sleep?

Can't I settle you down
and tell you the light
is not morning and, really Rosemary,
the ravenous birds singing

are not alive and hungry,
and the morning
not bringing up the sun
with both your two hands?

JOHN MOLE

Not About Roses
(to Mary)

I have never written
A poem about roses,
Supposing them
The thorniest subject –

How many before me
Have pricked their fingers
On what they thought
Was the only flower,

The one for love
Without really trying
Like the easiest word
To understand

Or a rhyme so exact
It would live for ever
In its cut-glass bowl
And not need water.

Harder than that
To say *I love you*
With the words still earthed
In a dusty soil

Which nevertheless
Is best for sunflowers
Though too dry for me
To do you justice

Or offer more
Than the curious drift
Of a loving poem
Not about roses.

PETER SCUPHAM

A Slice of Cake

I watched her sifting night and day
And soft and sweet into her bowl.
The air was full of harmless love
Which slipped her fingers: lights above,
Geraniums with their vixen smell
Beyond the glass. The past could say

Her hair was darkly tied, tell how
The sunshine flicked its cleansing tongue
About the room. Such lemon zest
For licking scraps! It did its best
To make the knives and glasses ring.
I had my cake, and ate it. Now,

My ghosts and I, too old to learn
New table-manners, ask for more
In voices bleached to white on white.
They match my hunger, bite for bite.
A day, a week, a month, a year –
They might have known I would return

To take her crumbs of comfort, wait
For grace: that gift of tongues I lost
Between her black and silver hair.
A second slice: to break and share
As if I still could find the taste
To finish up what's on my plate.

TED HUGHES

Flame

For oxygen mask
You had Green Farm, near Hexham.
The dusty chemistry
Of the bared, bedroom floorboards
Gave you enough, in a few breaths.
You brought it away. The salmon
Under the stained current of the North Tyne
Added a suspect ingredient –
The one, crucial grain of too-much.
But the rent was next to nothing, measured out
In exact proportion. And though the oracular book
Had to fall open at:
'Be absolute for death: either death or life . . .'
As if the Master himself had undersigned
A different contract, the Dower House at Park End
Was your back-up fail-safe –
The rent a guarantee and the only snag
A gardener for the paradisal gardens.
Manchester provided, as extras,
Bed coverlet and blankets, to muffle your ears
From any bang and limit any damage.
But climbing into the train at Manchester Central
With all that First Aid kit
And ali those protective devices
You did not know how history had already
Cast you to repeat itself.
You had no idea
What signed paper had found you at last
After so many years, what detonator
Waited in your flat
To include even your wildest hopes

As so much dirty cobalt
In its nuclear reaction –
Synchrony so precisely attuned
You barely had time to rip the envelope
And grab for the telephone
Before it was all over.

SIMON RAE

Summit

Summoned, I travelled north to find you.
But you were away over the white wastes
The regular stride of your breathing

Beyond all possible distraction,
The eyes above the mask snow-blinded,
Fixed on the unimaginable distant peak.

At base camp they served tea and biscuits
All night. You laboured on right through
That night, the next day, and through most

Of the next night's biscuit ration,
Until, sometime in the mid-nothing
Of the endless hour that summed up all the rest,

You reached the summit with a final
Floundering gasp, and stuck
Your flag through both our waiting hearts.

Inheritance

It glinted on your finger all my life,
Clicked on your whiskey glass or the steering wheel.
You used to take it off to wash your face
In restaurant gents before we had a meal.

The seal's a warlike claymore in a fist –
Though you were the most peaceable of men,
At peace with The Bookseller and your pipe.
It could though, at a glance, look like a pen.

And that's how I prefer to look at it,
A great plumed ink-primed quill
– Although I type, and my first book of poems
Was published just too late for you to sell.

LAWRENCE SAIL

Acts Of Will

Father, son and daughter strapped
Like dummies into our rearing seats,
We are together in the 'plane
By an act of will entitled
The Family's Last Holiday Before
The Fledglings Fly The Nest.

And the aeroplane itself is one
Colossal dream of an iron will –
Shuddering to overcome
Every instinct of gravity,
Lifting what must fall, compressing
What must fly apart.

High up, the sun stabs from blue:
In the children's eyes, a bright joy
As they survey beneath us
Rumpled duvets of cloud.
How shall I not bring us all down
With the dull weight in my heart?

When we land, I know it is
By an act of will called simply
Not Yet, that my children
Do not walk away for ever,
Or dismiss the pretence of landing here
At the time that we left home.

ROGER CRAWFORD

An Eighteenth Century Childhood

When I waf a fmall, fmall boy
I ufed to go to fleep
fometimef my fleep waf fhallow
and fometimef my fleep waf deep

Awake! Arife! my fifter cried
Af fwiftly af you can!
we've porridge in the pot
And fome bacon in the pan!

Ah! let me fwoon abed and reft
Af found af other nipperf!
Arife! fhe cried; with fwollen eyef
I fought round for my flipperf

47

GRACE NICHOLS

Your Own Content

(For Kalera, my baby daughter)

You are full of your own content.
Fingers gripping affirmation,
Round my index.

Eyes, two steady worlds,
Holding me
In their unjudging axis of light.

Sometimes, you're a screeching otter.
Sometimes, a sunflower,
The stem of your neck can hardly hold.

Sometimes, you're a clean piglet.
Swinging you upwards from your bath,
My back aches.

Though you may or may not remember,
These godful days
Will set your tone – forever.

Weather Forecast

How it kyan snow so
How it kyan cold so
How it kyan fog so
How it kyan frost so

How it kyan rain so
How it kyan hail so
How it kyan damp so
How it kyan dark so

Is how it hard so.

E A MARKHAM

On Explaining The Result Of The Race To Your Mother

Her eyes are bad; you can't take refuge
in that: her sons erect on the podium
receiving medals for running and jumping
have to be acknowledged. Why *them*, you think,
with a rash of jealousy lotioned
into something more presentable: they
chasing the wind, leaping the bar, have stretched
your mind, too, past comfort. So why not *us*, nearer
home, greyer, trailing in another pack but clutching
goodies made visible by our words? The old arguments
are too heavy for mind alone to shift. The mother's
eyes see past this snub: three sons (not strangers)
same face, accent, each with a national
anthem not her own. There were times, it's true,
when men left home to build in foreign
lands, and scattered seed where no one knew.
A few decades reapprenticed to the world and we've shifted
view on what's good and not good to know: there are
no bastards in this family now grown large
by claiming its own. But the flags
held aloft by children fingering medals
have nothing left of our cloth: will this extend
the emergency order of exile? A memory
fogs like cloud over those factories, farms unkind
to animals which bring protesters out on the street.
Ah yes. But remember, the sky over cruelty
can be blue: (So many flags show good weather!)
Let's watch the television; your distant sons
smile and wave. Daughters now. More flags. Gold
hung from necks more precious than the rest. And let's
not look at one another while we're being honoured.

50

JOHN HEATH-STUBBS

Pertinax Imperator

'Daddy, you must buy it!'
How his daughters, his daughters and his wife
Egged him on, 'You must buy it, Daddy!'
They meant, of course, the Roman Empire.

The Praetorian guard, having disposed
Of the last unlucky incumbent, had decided
To put the whole caboodle up for auction –
Sale to the highest bidder. He could afford it too.
He'd made his pile, this pertinacious man,
Exporting savoury fish sauce
To all the furthest provinces;
And from the blood and bruised backs of the slaves,
Groans of the starving poor.

The gavel struck. He paid down cash
(It jingled with a kind of hollow laughter),
Assumed the purple, made a few
Tedious speeches to the somnolent
And ineffectual Senate. Before the year was out
He'd gone the way of all the others. The Praetorians
Notched up another tally.

'The world at sale' – no, not really the world,
Merely the fringe of a Mediterranean fish pond.
In the high Andes, Guatemalan forests,
Beside the Yang-Tze or the Bramahputra,
Other great states, each one claiming
That it was universal, tottered onwards,
Oblivious of Rome, towards
Their own inevitable disintegration.

51

As for his wife and daughters, I don't suppose
History has any news of them.
I like to think that they perhaps retired
To the Roman equivalent of a private hotel
In some salubrious resort – Baiae for instance –
And bored the other guests with detailed anecdotes
About the reign of mighty Pertinax.
We only know of it distilled,
A few brief sentences
Where we may savour Gibbon's irony,
While still great empires fall about our ears.

GEORGE SZIRTES

Chinese White

(From 'Bridge Passages')

Do you remember that scene in *Ashes and Diamonds* where
the hero rushes forward through the clotheslines and bleeds
to death among the sheets? Or was it
in *Canal* (I can't remember now.) A square
of white turns slowly red. The redness fades
to black and white. The picture is a composite,

a form of poster. The War, the Resistance,
something about betrayal, all mixed up
in a child's mind who didn't see
the war, for whom it is a haunting presence
of sheets and blood. An image hangs and drops
in a grey passageway or alley.

His name was Zbigniew, and he wore dark glasses,
and later he jumped from a train (a true life fact)
because, well, Poles are like that,
they get drunk, morose, etcetera. The girl who kisses
the boy was blonde as always. Was it an act
of bravery him getting shot

or cowardice? We could look it up in books
but that is not the point (we pull our serious face)
but something in the falling, the how
and where of it. And so wherever one looks
the same old images return and find their place,
a square, an alleyway, a row

of ordinary houses suddenly still and hot
and people falling lying as if on a square
of film. You see the victim's head
as someone aims and shoots him, and you cut
to tanks or bodies or a sheet hung out to air,
a white square slowly turning red.

PETER ROBINSON

Leaf-viewing

Autumn's end, this was the season
for some looking back and forward.

Elsewhere old régimes were falling.
Party men and Presidents fled.

Open thoughts, fresh feelings, fruit
and veg, consumer durables

were wanted; coal trains setting out
might reach their destinations.

In aid of what the others wanted
certain streets were caked in blood.

Among part-intelligible signs I'd stood
deciphering brands and, was it?, *murder*.

As the *walk–don't walk* light changed
still a Chinese demonstration,

vociferous, under escort, came on,
merged with forward-swarming crowds

of Sunday shoppers in Shibuya:
'You a student?' 'No, a teacher.'

'Many teachers died there too.'
Words of peaceful intermingling

had re-echoed through the year:
you've lived in interesting times.

Across a wintry hemisphere
our separated fates converge.

Seasonal differences each endures,
each slight thaw and freeze.

There were pieces of misfortune
painted red still clinging to the trees.

Autumn 1989

ANTHONY THWAITE

Freedom

Through the vast crowded wards, thousands came round.
Limbs twitched; mouths opened, uttering strange old cries;
Wild smiles and tears, and snarls at what went on
Through decades of paralysis.
                              Bodies are found
Strewn in the corridors. A doctor lies
Battered in blood. The warders have all gone,
Savaged by patients who woke up to see
The doors were open. Healers are unmasked
As torturers; nurses crucified
When drugs, withdrawn, reveal them all to be
Captors and guards.
                    And those who this way died
Are faceless as their patients.
                                And some asked
How the great hospital would care for those
Who lie there still, free, in a deep repose.

Gairaigo*

Sitting in apāto
Quiet in my manshon
I write this in my nōto,
Lacking a wāpuro.

I am on a tsuā
From faraway Yōroppa
Where I wear a toppā
Or ōbā in the winter.

Terebi and rajio
Speak to me Nihon-go.
Tabako, arukōru
Help my arubaito.

Invite me to a konpa,
Give me a haibōru,
I have no abekku . . .
Show me please the toiré.

Better fetch shaberu.
Now I need a beddo,
Feeling pretty ierō . . .
Ga-gi-gu-ge-go.

*Japanese 'words that come from outside'

apartment; mansion (block of flats); notebook; word-
processor; tour; Europe; topcoat; overcoat; television; radio;
cigarettes; alcohol; work (from G. arbeit); party; highball;
girl/boy-friend (from F. avec); toilet; shovel; bed; yellow.

NICK DRAKE

The Single Shoes Of Spain

The bridge is the gypsies' ceiling; every summer
they travel to the stones of this dry river
with the rag and bone of all the family
and set up residence, no door, no key.
The men stand at the bar; the women wash
the clothes, and lay them out on a thorn bush
and the hot stones, and then sit in the shade
to watch them dry. They have no money; trade
is what the river gives away; the scrap
the wealthy town dumps off the bridge. Cars drop
broken on the stones; cookers, burnt out,
a red armchair, some prams, a plastic bucket,
a doll's head, an umbrella. And the shoes,
the single shoes of Spain, those mysteries
of slipper, boot, stiletto without a pair,
useful only to the lottery seller
with two left feet, or a dancer with one leg;
eyes lacking laces, sole a broken tongue.
September, they move on to the winter bridges
leaving some shoes, and several empty fridges.

CAL CLOTHIER

Photograph From The Pindos Mountains, Northern Greece

The stones of the dried-up river bed
were large misshapen reptile eggs
whose white glare bullied the eye.

They drained the shadow under the bridge
of any darkness; its three arches
stood like ash that still retained its shape.

There was no road to the bridge
or from the bridge; it might have been
tossed into the air by an ancient flood;

it flowed above the river-bed
in three elegant waves of stone,
a monument to vanished water.

From the far bank the sound of bells –
two, twenty, dozens, hundreds of bells –
came over the bridge, and in its wake

ten, forty, seventy, a hundred goats,
a hundred goats flowing over the bright unbroken
triple wave of the luminous bridge.

The gamelan of a hundred goat bells
shimmered your hearing; turned the visible world
into an audible river of sound.

Here is the photograph I took: see how
the hot misshapen moons of stone
blazed into the camera first. See how

the undulating line of goats
is burned into the line of the bridge. The melody
of their movement is stillness.

ROBERT WELLS

The Iran-Iraq War

The roadside soft with dust, the threadbare hills,
The teahouse with its incongruous velvet couch,
The felt-capped boy stopping with his goats to stare:
Dusk drew these together in a frail coherence
As the moon rose, strengthening through deep-blue air.

In that dry numinous light, it seemed, the country
Lay changelessly far off, and the childish face
Unreachably open between domed cap and coat.
I count the years now to reckon the herdboy's age,
And guess the sequel. No village was too remote.

At Moonrise

Youth's good was its own body,
Which did not fail.
At moonrise I would dive naked
Into the pool,

Splinter the beams, surface,
Watch them regather.
Self-knowledge was no more
Than the touch of water.

KEN SMITH

The Chamber of Torment
from 'Three Venetian Pieces'

Outside men groan, caged in the square,
buried with their feet sticking up. In this room
the strappado has heard all their pleading,
the nailed planks have witnessed their replies.

It's all very simple: a plinth and a rope,
a long stem of agony hung from the roofbeam,
and the man drops, breaks, babbles whether he prays
hourly, at nightfall, or to the man in the moon.

Or what you wish, signors, I beg you
throw my brother in there behind the curtain,
take my friend Giovanni Giacomo who deserves it
for the money he's owed me these 15 centuries.

ANNE STEVENSON

Double Glazing

Trapped flies that hatch,
   buzzing between two spider-mottled panes,
drag their unnourished bodies up the glass.
   March sun makes prisms
   of their leaded wings
that grope for light webbed over with remains
   of ancestors whose
   frantic baby matings
ended in stills: a rain of shrivelled husks
   on a desert sill.

I could play god
   and set them free at will.

My mind's eye sees them
   soar from glassy doctrine
into the high and hallelujah air.
   To give them freedom:
unscrew that inward-looking cage,
reach through and push the outside
   open. Righteous rage.
   I half pause in despair
each time I pass the torture lesson
viewed from the whitewashed landing
   by the stair.

Binoculars In The Ardudwy

A lean season, March, for ewes
who, all winter, camped on the hills.
They're gathered in now to give birth
to children more cheerful than themselves.

There's the farmer, his jeep, a black dog,
trotting, now rolling on his back.
At the gate, sheep bunched – one alone
drifting down the steep Cambrian track.

Look now, the sun's reached out,
painting turf over ice-smoothed stone.
A green much younger than that
praises Twll Nant and Penisa'r Cwm.

All this through the lens of a noose
I hold to my focusing eyes,
hauling hill, yard, barn, man, house
and a line of blown washing across

a mile of diluvian marsh.
I see every reed, rust-copper,
and a fattened S-bend of the river.
Then, just as I frame it, the farm

wraps its windows in lichenous weather
and buries itself in its tongue.
Not my eye but my language is wrong
And the cloud is between us forever.

Under cover of mist and myth
the pieced fields whisper together,
'Find invisible Maesygarnedd . . .
Y Llethr . . . Foel Ddu . . . Foel Wen.'

P J KAVANAGH

The Permanent Question

At the back of the hall of the head the permanent question:
Do the now-become-lovely, the unimpeded,
If they exist at all, still help us?
Avert, if they can, with magical palm, the car-crash?
Prevent, with a palm reversed, on the dangerous kerb?
Or even, like mothers chatting outside a playground,
Impossibly adult, more concerned with each other,
Are patting our heads with invisible, unfelt palms
And, over our heads, call skirt-cling, 'Just a stage!'

When patient beasts lift up their heads from feeding
We see in alerted eyes an identical question,
'Am I safe?' We recognise their expression
With greater fellow-feeling than we know
And try to pat their heads. They run away.
Left to endure the grip of night alone
(For who in his senses goes to join the sheep)
They are there in the morning, frost-caked,
Night-stunned, with no choice. They raise their heads.

January Evening

It is the métier and, after all, self-chosen,
To waste a day and fail to find expression
For morning's special frisk, the way brass trees
Leaped from ribbed ground, and one-side frozen
Molehills werc white-breasted, like still plovers:
To know the harsh imperative to praise,
Not to placate a god who made these treasures,
Without a motive, save necessity's.

And not one word, of fear, of jubilation
At a quick, kind unveiling, no good word spoken:
Of fear, because the page bears no true mark
And light is lost. But never lost, the soul's
Necessity to praise, and hills of moles,
White-breasted, still as plovers, roost in dark.

D J ENRIGHT

Demonstration

And when we are born
When we are airborne
An inscrutable being
Shows how in an emergency
We should put on a life-jacket
In a few simple movements
Head through there, tie the tapes
Together, and tighten thus
Then pull the plastic knob to inflate
But only when you are safely outside.

The demonstration is hurried and
Perfunctory, not easy to interpret
While you are still inside your life.

In High Dudgeon

The air is thin around here; and so are skins. Ringed with
ranks of tall offences, towering piques and impenetrable
umbrage, it's not a good place for the elderly. As they
linger along the affront or trudge testily up the rebuffs,
they talk of taking recumbency and moving to Low Dudgeon.
A dank, depressed area, known only for its grovel pits and
humble pies – they'd soon succumb to sinking feelings.

DAVID CONSTANTINE

Clare Leaves High Beach

Others also were muttering and went
Each alone on the designated ways
Tipping their headgear. Said Doctor Allen,
His kind keeper, for such men
The best company in the world is trees.

Turmoil in the head, tempest: a beech
With its arms ripped off, the yellow bone
Showing, rags everywhere, the shriek
Of roots in air, and the mind reached
Into the crippling. He bolted then, for home.

Lay down, beat, his head the needle
North for the morning, he lay between
His two wives quietly and the love was equalled.
Woke. They were gone. The sadness welled
Out of the ground and through his eyes again.

A face came over him, it had a crown
That bulged from some rags of hair, a face
As large and a dome as bald as the moon
Beamed down at him. It was his own:
Good-natured, cheerful, and quite crazed.

He lay for the north. Out of him travelled,
As though he bled, the love of certain trees
In place, a spire, a stile, a golden field,
Lapwing in thousands. How much he held
And must crawl after now on hands and knees!

Under That Bag Of Soot

Under that bag of soot, when I moved it,
Something had been trying to grow. The light,
They think, as soon as the earth warms. Eyelessly
Start pushing. Then to be flattened and on the belly
Have to go feeling for help . . . Sunlight,

The gift of singing comes back to the birds,
And the things that had been doing their best to grow
Get up, they are white, they are a damaged yellow.
Nobody will ask such things to flower, only
To turn a decent green. A man like that

Released into the community with a shaved head
And the marks of fangs on his temples stands
Every day at the lights and when the green man shows
And everybody hurries he stands still, through red
And the next green he stands there like

Caspar on the asphalt with his wounded feet
And one little scrap of speech: that what
He wanted was to be a rider, but
He could smell the dead still growing in the soil
And the green he needed made him vomit.

The gardener of all this raises a merciful spade.

C H SISSON

Deep-rooted Fears

Deep-rooted fears
– Should not fears have deep roots? –
And terrifying love
Send their pale shoots above
The surface where no other growth appears.

Expect no more,
Though other men will live, and women too,
To see out time and witness its distress
And what in us grows less
May grow again as it has grown before.

O barren age! whose trust is all in lies;
Others have known what you no longer know:
Hope backwards, you may find
The speed of a slow mind
Dawdling eternally before surprise.

Wonder there must be which is not short
Or long, nor has any dimension.
Can you find that? I say
That there in night shone day
Although I know it only by report.

Leave hope, leave fear, attend to what is,
The smallest thing that is is better than
The best that can be said,
And a man dead
Finds more than we in our short silences.

Muchelney Abbey

The quiet flood
Lies between hedges and turns back the light,
Black and blue like the bruises of the time
– Sheet after sheet of record where the crime
Is lost beneath the water. Rushes write
Illegibly in mud

And willows point
Downward without weeping, or else raise
Flourishing heads topping gigantic trunks.
Uneasily the shadows of dead monks
Move past the abbey in which no-one prays.
Who will anoint

The wounds they did not,
More than we do ourselves, attempt to cure?
Grey evening behind which the sun, unseen,
Sets to the sound of church-bells, which still mean
No more than echoes: and, for sure,
Nature will rot.

O come away
To death O human race! Accept no more
This watery world in which the fox and hare
Have lost their scent, in which the livid air
Promises nothing on this wasted shore
But closing day

Yet spring may come,
Who knows? with drought and terror, or else flowers,
For time may circle back, once more pretend
A grammar of renewal without end,
A summer with its vacuum of bright hours
When all is dumb.

CHARLES TOMLINSON

At Bob Lucid's Place

There was enough of summer
in the autumn
to fill the entire afternoon
with sunlit colour,

and there was enough
of silence in the room
to lighten the burden of the city
as it filtered in

through curtains the air kept shifting,
raising among the leaves
of a magazine
tiny tidal sounds

as it breathed them open
and shut them again:
this pulse kept clear
a fluctuating frontier

between the room
and the traffic of feet
and cars negotiating
the intersection on the street

that awaited us,
the shadows of passers-by
advancing eagerly out of a sun
casting them forward from its blaze on the horizon.

FLEUR ADCOCK

Wren-Song

How can I prove to you
that we've got wrens in the garden?

A quick flick of a tail
in or out of the ivy hedge
is all you'll ever see of them;

and anyway, I'm asleep.
Not dreaming, though: I can hear him,
the boss-wren, out there in the summer dawn –

his bubbling sequences,
an octave higher than a blackbird's,
trickling silver seeds into my ears.

I'll get the tape-recorder.
But no, it's in another room,
and I've no blank tapes for it;

and anyway, I'm asleep.
Hard to wake up, after a sultry night
of restless dozing, even for the wren.

I've tracked his piccolo solo
in the light evenings, from hedge to apple tree
to elder, sprints of zippy flight in between.

I've looked him up: 'A rapid
succession of penetrating and jubilant
trills, very loud for so small a bird.'

I'll get the tape-recorder.
I'll find an old cassette to record over.
I'm getting up to fetch it now –

but no, I'm still asleep;
it was a dream, the getting up.
But the wren's no dream. It *is* a wren.

IRELAND

MATTHEW SWEENEY

Digging

Out in the park two children are digging,
two girls, their long hair wind-tossed and free.
They are making little headway
although they lean with all their might.
Someone ought to tell them their flat shovel
is not the tool. Someone ought to take
that blown-off branch still sprouting leaves
that lies on the ground by their feet
and start a bonfire with it, let loose
its green smoke. Someone ought to say
it's too frail and long to plant,
too late to set. But the two girls keep digging,
with the mother-trunk firm above them,
and behind, the one lamp in the street still on.

His Dog

Where is this dog he sees and I can't?
Why is he pointing to the window,
then beckoning me to rise from bed
and herd his sheep back to the hills?
All around me sick men sleep through
his hissed commands, his tearing cries
that the night-nurse runs to calm –

a calm that night-lights can't prolong,
or daylight either, though his daughters
when they come with wills that lack
his signature, don't get a sound
or a move from him, don't get the farm,
although they plead and squabble.
Where is his dog now, where is it?

EAVAN BOLAND

What We Lost

It is a winter afternoon.
The hills are frozen. Light is failing.
The distance is a crystal earshot.
A woman is mending linen in her kitchen.

She is a countrywoman.
Behind her cupboard doors she hangs sprigged,
stove-dried lavender in muslin.
Her letters and mementos and memories

are packeted in satin at the back with
gaberdine and worsted and
the cambric she has made into bodices;
the good tobacco silk for Sunday Mass.

She is sewing in the kitchen.
The sugar-feel of flax is in her hands.
Dusk. And the candles brought in then.
One by one. And the quiet sweat of wax.

There is a child at her side.
The tea is poured, the stitching put down.
The child grows still, sensing something of importance.
The woman settles and begins her story.

Believe it, what we lost is here in this room
on this veiled evening:
The woman finishes. The story ends.
The child, who is my mother, gets up, moves away.

In the winter air, unheard, unshared,
the moment happens, hangs fire, leads nowhere.
The light will fail and the room darken,
the child fall asleep and the story be forgotten.

The fields are dark already.
The frail connections have been made and are broken.
The dumb-show of legend has become language,
is becoming silence and who will know that once

words were possibilities and disappointments,
were scented closets filled with love-letters
and memories and lavender hemmed into muslin,
stored in sachets, aired in bed-linen;

and travelled silks and the tones of cotton
tautened into bodices, subtly shaped by breathing;
were the rooms of childhood with their griefless peace,
their hands and whispers, their candles weeping brightly?

Distances

The radio is playing downstairs in the kitchen.
The clock says eight and the light says
winter. You are pulling up your hood against a bad morning.

Don't leave, I say. Don't go without telling me
the name of that song. You call it back to me from the stairs:
'I wish I Was In Carrickfergus'

and the words open out with emigrant grief the way the streets
of a small town open out in
memory: salt-loving fuchsias to one side and

a market in full swing on the other with
linen for sale and tacky apples and a glass and wire hill
of spectacles on a metal tray. The front door bangs

and you're gone. I will think of it all morning while a fine
drizzle closes in, making the distances
fiction: not of that place but this and of how

restless we would be, you and I, inside the perfect
music of that basalt and sandstone
coastal town. We would walk the streets in

the scentless and flawless afternoon of a ballad measure,
longing to be able
to tell each other that the starched lace and linen of

adult handkerchiefs scraped your face and left your tears
falling; how the apples were mush inside the crisp sugar
shell and the spectacles out of focus.

JOHN HUGHES

The Rafters

On the eve of his thirteenth birthday
Fitz stood at Doyle's Corner
Watching a team of shooting stars
Plough across the August sky.

He gritted his teeth and wished
That sky would miraculously peel back
To reveal the huge oak rafters
He had dreamt held it in place.

It was the last wish of his childhood.

The next day he was given a telescope.

That night he could see nothing for clouds.

DENNIS O'DRISCOLL

1989

Peking students on their black bikes:
shoals wavering through river-wide squares,
merging and separating in the sun,
fish that test the purity of a habitat . . .
They remind me of schoolgoing cyclists
in my childhood, chains clenching their teeth
for the final assault on Liberty Square.
(That was Thurles in the late sixties,
Mao's book colouring the thoughts
of a few red-headed pupils
gathered at the '98 Rebellion statue,
its flag trailing like a winged victory).

Tiananmen Square was cleared by guns,
flagged with an indelible message of blood.
On Wenceslas Square, crowds cheered Havel
as the guard changed, bringing relief
to the banned philosophers, night watchmen,
who had waited for the light to dawn.
All was quiet on Liberty Square in this year
of revolutions, just a few lads in drunken dispute
coming from the Chinese take-away
or my young brother, Declan, and his friends
told by a policeman to move on,
not to disturb the peace of sleepy residents

with their discussion of world affairs.

NUALA Ní DHOMHNAILL

Breith Anabai Thar Lear

Luaimnigh do shíol i mo bhroinn,
d'fháiltíos roimh do bhreith.
Dúrt go dtógfainn go cáiréiseach thú
de réir gnása mo nuamhuintire.

An leabhar beannaithe faoi do philiúr
arán is snáthaid i do chliabhán,
léine t'athar anuas ort
is ag do cheann an scuab urláir.

Bhí mo shonas
ag cur thar maoil
go dtí sa deireadh
gur bhris na bainc
is sceith
frog deich seachtainí;
ní mar a shíltear a bhí.

Is anois le teacht na Márta
is an bhreith a bhí
le bheith i ndán duit
cuireann ribíní bána na taoide
do bhindealáin i gcuimhne dom,
tointe fada na hóinsí.

Is ní raghad
ag féachaint linbh
nuabheirthe mo dhlúthcharad
ar eagla mo shúil mhillteach
do luí air le formad.

NUALA Ní DHOMHNAILL
(translated by Bob Welch)

Premature Birth Overseas

Your seed darted in my womb,
I welcomed your birth.
I said I'd raise you according to
the customs of my new relations:

the holy book under your pillow,
a needle and a loaf in your cradle,
over you your father's shirt,
the scrubbing brush by your head.

My joy
was overflowing
until at last
the ramparts burst
and a ten week old frog
broke out.

Now with March come round
and the birth-time here
which was laid down for you
the white ribbons of the sea,
tedious windings of despair,
remind me of your swaddling clothes.

I won't go to see
my friend's newborn child
for fear my evil eye
would light on it with hate.

ROBERT JOHNSTONE

Postcard From London

The cherry and magnolia
have arrived already,
unexpected visitors
like us, exotic species.

When I go out the next-door cat
(the only creature on the street
to whom we say hello)
tracks me to the shops.

He's got a knack of slipping through
the railings like a skein of smoke
as if no line divided
neighbour from frosty neighbour.

I wish I had such style,
fluent at translation
from northern into southern or
from winter into sudden spring.

Factory Fortnight

Who'd feel at home in the Aero room,
that desert of surfaces, tiles and glass,
angles from a geometer's dream?

Not a soul disturbs the peace
of six machines which softly stir
alone for week on week

turning and turning each of their colours,
piping them up in viscous circles,
dripping them back over and over.

Trays are waiting to form the bars;
humans will lift them on to racks
inside banks of vacuum chambers.

The Aero people loved straight lines
but were inspired by circles,
bubbles exploding, endless rotations.

The Aero people are gone forever
leaving only their concept of time,
their circumspection, their endless measure.

PETER McDONALD

The Hands Of Juán Peron

It was going to take four of us at least:
one to kill the floodlights and blind
the cameras whirring at their posts,
another to slip out from behind
the thick-set line of trees and past
the guards' hut, moving from lock to lock
with the quick fingers of a surgeon;
then, and this is where I came in,
for dragging the lead far enough back
from the roof of his bunker coffin,
the services of two or three strong men.

They had set the date for early June,
mentioning things like a rising curve,
a jump in the temperature, tides
having to be taken on the turn;
knowing they'd have reasons of their own
as well as reputations to preserve,
all I could do was set a modest price
and say that a poor man sees both sides
no matter what the question;
I told them I never ignored advice;
and yes, I'd always forget a face.

The night, when it came, was thick with heat,
settled alike over moonless slums
and the new road, lighted and straight,
that led to the gates and the big trees
swaying at the edge of his estate;
even here, there was the city noise,
and insects, and faint clicks and hums

that came from the gateman's intercom;
beneath us, twigs and gravel gave
the tiniest hints of our presence:
just after midnight, we made our move.

Everything was happening at long distance:
there were maybe fifty or sixty yards
between me and that mausoleum
(a wedding-cake in black marble,
solid, swollen up with importance),
as I watched the first of two guards
go down, and one man sidle
up to the locked door of the tomb;
he knelt there like a pilgrim
for a matter of seconds, then gave the sign
to bring us out into the open.

Just like in dreams where you run for miles
uphill, towards or away from something,
we were up and into the dead hall
with its musty drapes and flags, its tiles
running cold beneath us all along
the polished path to his resting place.
We climbed the casket like a wall;
a tiny spotlamp had been left on
for a nightlight, and as we looked down
we saw him lying where it shone,
a child in bed, with a waxy face.

From behind us there were shouted whispers,
and a tool-bag slung up and caught;
I was pulling him out by the epaulettes,
until his stuffed corpse with its taut
dried skin, its coiffure and powdered whiskers,
was sitting straight again; I brought

the two hands up from underneath
the lid; they were stained from cigarettes
but otherwise clean, stone-dry and brittle.
I blew, and chemicals under my breath
rose, then fell, as dust might settle.

The hacksaw was out and into his wrist
that minute, rasping its way through flesh
as though it had been dry paper; the rest
was simple, snapping bones like chalk
then whipping his light hand off in a flash
and into a cushioned box; the right hand first
and then the left, the two laid flush,
wrapped over, and the lid jammed on.
We disappeared without needing to talk,
going our own ways, one by one,
taking with us the hands of Juán Peron.

Before we left I handed over a box
to the silent men who had stood behind me,
watching, refining whatever their plans were;
too clever really to spot a hoax,
which is what they were given. I'm holed up here
in this tiny room where they'll never find me,
waiting until the right moment lands
like a dove with an idea in its beak,
to put me in the money. So now, inside the Ark,
I'm left with the main chance, food for a week,
a telephone, and a clean pair of hands.

WALES

CHRISTINE EVANS

Lighthouse Keeper

Inside's gloss-painted like a hospital.
The radio stammers, blurts, then hums.
Sport or men with guns mutter on a screen
All look at, no-one watches, in an acrid haze
Of Players' Number 6 or roll-your-owns.
Nestle's Milk coffee or with white lumps floating
Is the only sign in here that you're offshore
(Formica buckling, tin teapot, pedal bin)
Till you catch reflections of the symmetry
Of nursery tale – for there are three
Of everything – three chairs with thin foam
Cushions that slide down as soon
As sat on, three tea-towels, and bookshelves;
Out in the garden, three lavatory cells
Three toolsheds, pigsties, garden plots gone wild

And three pale unfocused sedentary men
Sleeping, eating, being awake
On or off according to a roster.

Bas steps out, shirt-sleeved, to do the Met
(which numbers on the weather form he'll tick)
Acres of white foam, the air
A wide blue yawn he slams in from:
Christ! It's cold enough out there –
Their laughter drowns the throb of engines.

But sometimes, he's confided, in the small hours
Snecking the white gate close behind him
He truants, leaving light in its tower cage
Where homing seabirds grunt and scream and fall

To tread salt turf springy with old roots
And stand like a captain in the wind
Reading the dark stretch of his deck
Sensing the night miles crossed
Till his heartbeat's only a flicker
His cigarette a brave red throb
On the seabed of the floating stars.

His daylight brain thinks it forgotten
But in off-duty dreams, a hundred miles
From sea, he feels the island dip and steady;
Glimpses the dark walls building, pushed astern
Tumbling, crawling, gathering, re-gathering
Outrun, but following.

TIM LIARDET

The Water-Garden

The zoological squeaks of perambulators pass.
Down and round to the Water-garden go the long steps.
Chipped statues, on worn patches of the grass,
Hold utterly still the bird-bath that rescinds
An offer of water, shrunk to a stain in the heat.
Rigid Noah outstares the fountain's drops:
The bronze discolours, as the four embodied winds
Divide their separate powers about his feet.

The drops fly, bubble in deluge, and dissipate.
What is it, then, that eludes? Everything
Offers up the emblem of its shifting state.
Ephemeral the squabble of sparrows bathing;
The tree can grow no further inside its cramped cage;
The bubbles cling, or tremble, volatile.
A far roar pumps up a disonnected rage.
The empty pool implies the crocodile.

STEVE GRIFFITHS

The Chiming At Trwyn Du

Brilliant as oiled plumage in hollows of sand
at first, the cars' paint
fades in the salt breeze
while their humans peel off into solitude.
The crest of the waves' surge is unbroken,
and the running of the silence is crowned
by the bell off Trwyn Du.
God's cry contracts to a hum
that fades in the current,
there, and there, he cannot
leave it alone, the loud
irregular call of a secretive bird.
There is no passage landward:
we watch, blessed, from the rocks
in the company of the deep-wrinkled mountains.

GILLIAN CLARKE

Swimming With Seals

Two horizons:
a far blue line
where a ship diminishes,
and the evening sun lets slip;
and submarine,
where we glimpse stars and shoals
and shadowy water-gardens
of what's beyond us.

When the seal rises
she rests her chin on the sea
as we do, and tames us with her gaze.
On shore, beside their cars,
the elderly bask at the edge
of what they've lost,
and shade their eyes,
and lift binoculars.

She's gone,
apt to the sea's grace,
to watch us underwater from her place,
you with your mask and fins
strolling the shallow gardens of the sea,
me, finding depth
with a child's flounder of limbs,
hauling downwards on our chains of breath.

For a moment,
the old, looking out to sea,
all earth's weight beneath their folding chairs,
see only flawless blue to the horizon,

while we, in seconds of caught air,
swim down against buoyancy
to roll in amnion
like her September calf.

HILARY LLEWELLYN-WILLIAMS

The Sealwife

One day I shall find my skin again:
my own salt skin, folded dark, its fishweed stink
and tang, its thick warm fat, great thrusting tail

all mine: and I'll take it and shake it out
to the wind, draw it over me cool and snug,
laugh softly, and slip back to my element.

I shall find my stolen skin, hidden by you
for love (you said) that night the sea-people danced
stashed in some cleft in the rocks where I may not go

but used to go, and dance too, stepping free
in my new peeled body, the stalks of my legs in the moon-
light strange, my long arms shaping the sky

that have narrowed their circles down
to the tasks of these forked hands: lifting,
fetching, stirring, scrubbing, embracing – the small

stiff landlocked movements. In the sea
I plunged and swam for my own joy, sleek and oiled,
and I loved at will in rolling-belly tides.

Here love is trapped between the walls of a house
and in your voice and eyes, our children's cries;
whose boundaries I've understood, a language

learnt slowly, word by word. You've been dear and good –
how you would sing to me, those wild nights!
– and oil my breasts by firelight, and dip down

to taste my sea-fluids. I'd forget to mourn
those others then, trawling the flickering deeps.
Now I cry for no reason, and dream of seals:

an ocean booms in the far cave of my ear
and voices tug at me as I stand here
at the window, listening. Our children sleep

and by daylight they run from me. Their legs
strong, their backs straight, bodies at ease
on solid ground – though they play for hours on the shore

between sand and sea, and scramble the wet rocks
gladly. It won't be long now, the waiting:
they love to poke and forage in the cracks

of the cliffs; sharpeyed, calling, waving.

JEAN EARLE

Elegy

Winter is bone and brace.
With a frost courage I range –
Open the unused rooms
Where now no children sleep,
No more my parents come
To hang their garments,
Scented with home.

These shoes moulder,
Stuck up with paint. How many years
Since the kitchen was that colour!

Perpetual looking back
Does not do. Winter must freeze.
Freeze, then –
How is their absence different
From any other – say, loss of seed
That might have been sons.
Snapshots of all the dogs
We ever had, shuffled as one – but oh!
'The first shall be last and the last first'
Is true of dogs
As of people we have loved . . .

Chairs bagged in human shapes,
Curtains where the dogs
Encumbered hems, sprang out in velvet,
Sending up their eyes . . .

Close the doors now, let winter freeze.

Consider Lenin – who was death to thousands –
At home at any time,
In his glass room,
Successfully frozen. Even to him
Doors shut and the grey pilgrims
Cease to come.

A Dream

I am a girl again –
At home, where dreams begin.
Looking from a room
To the shaded verandah. My father there,
Talking to a young man,
The sunny garden behind them.

It seems that this visitor returns
From an absence. Before he went
There had been, as it were, a flower
Opening between us – no more than leaf
Around the promise of light.

We meet. With an unsure gesture
I offer something saved or obtained for him
While he was away. My other hand
Moves towards his, in formal greeting.

And we look at each other . . .

Like the flower: of an unknown colour
Till the air broaches it.

As an opening flower –
Only a vision of the bright stemful,
Later. Perhaps: if the air is kind.

MENNA ELFYN

Coch Yr Aeron

llygaid coch gan drallod
yw'r dwrglos dorf ar dir,
eu crwyn caled yn sgleinio
wrth i sgien rhagfyr eu rhathu.

A chyndyn yw'r gwreiddiau
i ildio islaw'r gors,
ei sigldonnen yn baglu gwadnau
eu cuchio i gorneli.

A'r Nadolig hwn eto

edrydd fy nhad
am frwydr y ffrwyth-lu
cyn eu medi,

wrth iddynt grimpio ymylwe bwrdd,
mwydion ar gyfer gwledd
a'u casdrem arnom – o wres
lleuadau newydd, platiau gwyn.

y chwerw felys ffrwyth
a fu unwaith yn gwrido
tu ol i aeliau'r cloddiau.

MENNA ELFYN
(translated by the author)

Cranberries

Eyes, red with affliction
a close packed crowd on land;
their hardproof skin shine
despite December's raspings.

Stubborn are the roots
to yield, their acquaintance
the mire's skin tissue
squares out soles, sulking.

this Christmas once again

my father tells us
how with resistance
they were reaped,

as they crease our table,
stewed just for a feast,
scowling at us from the warmth
of new moons, white plates.

the bitter sweet fruit,
that once blushed behind
the brow of hedgerows.

JOHN ORMOND

Family Matters

for his grand-daughter born on his birthday

When my father would have been 98
Soon, soon I was 98 with him. When a century
Went by I was alongside.

When he was a million years of age
I would be abreast (glaciers move strangely),
Brother in nothing and everything.

'Don't be long,' he'd say, going up to bed,
Slipping his shoes off, having banked the fire,
'Don't stay down too long.'

But now this added bud, this rose sprung
Out of ice, this jewel, this abundance, this certain
Renewal of my birthday. This gift breathes

For the first time, cries her first cries,
Suckles her mother's nestling composure in
Her Katherine, Katie, *bella Katerina*;

New sweetling, silver's newest wafer,
Infant of my new infancy, sipper of beginnings,
Fallen into the ancient blessings

Of the old air's wine. I am this infant's
Infant, sudden beholder of origins,
The inventor, seeing them, of the first skies;

As soon, anew, my father lays his dust
Upon my shoulder, blesses with me the bond, the solace
For turning back to the flung seedcorn of stars.

LESLIE NORRIS

Old Men

My grandfather could whistle like a bird.
His lips smiled beneath his white moustache,
and a wavering sibilance, a sound a bird might make
if it were far away and out of sight,
would hesitate about the kitchen. And,
There it is, he'd cry. We'd follow the unseen bird,
robin, he'd say, or thrush, among the dresser shelves
beyond his pointing finger, behind
the willow pattern plates in four cracked rows.
The bird sang round the room and then away.
You were too slow, he'd say, it's flown away.
We perched in a line on the horse-hair couch
and played along, because he liked that bird.
And once or twice I very nearly saw it.
Often, he'd have a real bird, some garden accident,
or baby fallen from its nest too young,
recovering in a cage with a wire front.
He'd feed it milky pap from an egg-spoon.

One Saturday we carried bricks from the fallen steelworks,
just he and I and four bricks on each journey,
harsh local oblongs, baked in fires long quenched.
We needed forty-two to edge his path.
I chose the ones we'd use, lifted my share.
My shirt was pink with gritty dust.
All day I nudged them into soldiers' lines,
bedding them in soil, using my grandfather's trowel,
his spirit-level, my fingers sore from rough surfaces.
For weeks I walked the path in the clear mornings,
seeing all well with my work. The fifth brick
from the end was marred, a black stain marred it.

After his death new people bought the house,
threw out our bricks. They lay for years
a slack heap, in a corner of the field.

It was seeing those old codgers,
those two old boys sitting on a park bench,
brought back my quiet grandfather.
They might have moved the world when young,
for all I knew, but there they were,
in the heavy gravity of their years,
talking in single words, the sentences
all spent. I walked for an hour
the gravel paths, admiring their certainty.

Something had given to those old men
more than endurance. They sat in calmness,
and watched the evening falling all around them,
although I could not see it.

ROBERT MINHINNICK

The Swift

The hall is cold, the stairwell dark,
And in my hand the brandy glass
Warm as a child's brow.
I answer the eleventh ring
And hear my question, furred with wine,
Its tiny echo fading like
A lightbulb's filament.

This is the sound the radio makes
When the anthem is played at midnight
And then engulfed by the inaudible
Electric breath between stars.
There's no-one there, no human voice
Describing why it telephones
At this desperate hour for telephones.

But I sit with my hot disc
Of liquor and listen to the fever
Of static, the racing brain-code
Of it that listens to me, and notices
The quickening pulse in my temple
Where the telephone is pressed,
The prickling of my hair.

And I overhear my car outside
Cooling like the brush of moths
Against a shade. This is the voice
Of dust that settles on its empire,
The sound that left my hand tonight
When I picked the swift,
Like a fallen evening-glove,

Dying from the road,
And spread its black crescent
Upon my palm. The weight of a glass.
But now the air tightens
To a straightjacket around the heart.
And three words like maroons explode
Hard inside the ear.

   Are
They ask. And hugely wait.
     You
– A Saharan interval.
      Happy?
And there's a desert in that voice
Come to me from the end of the world.
Now the brandy's hot as a test-tube,
Its perfume clotting in my throat,
And slapping the wall this hand can't find the switch.

R S THOMAS

Migrants

He is that great void
we must enter, calling
to one another on our way
in the direction from which
he blows. What matter
if we should never arrive
to breed or to winter
in the climate of our conception?

Enough we have been given wings
and a needle in the mind
to respond to his bleak north.
There are times even at the Pole
when he, too, pauses in his withdrawal,
so that it is light there all night long.

Contrary

When we are weak, we are
strong. When our eyes close
on the world, then somewhere
within us the bush

burns. When we are poor
and aware of the inadequacy
of our table, it is to that,
uninvited, the guest comes.

114